TO:

FROM:

W0115814

Published by Sourcebooks Casablanca, an imprint of Sourcebooks, Inc.
P.O. Box 4410, Naperville, Illinois 60567-4410
(630) 961-3900
Fax: (630) 961-2168
www.sourcebooks.com

Printed and bound in the United States of America.
SP 10 9 8 7 6 5 4 3 2 1

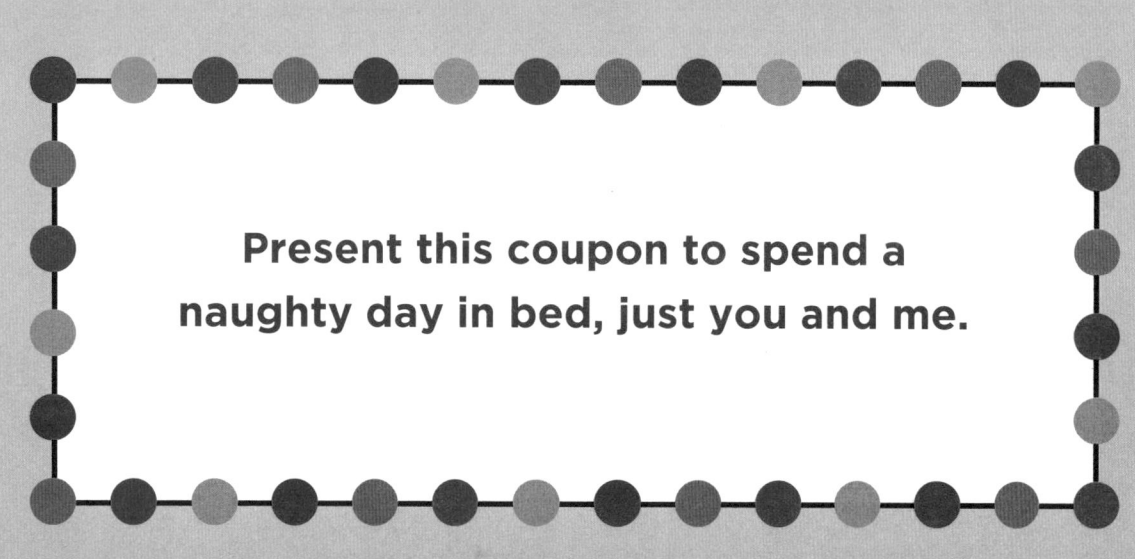

Present this coupon to spend a naughty day in bed, just you and me.

Booty call: This coupon is good for a quick and sexy rendezvous. Just call, and I'll come.

Redeem this coupon and I'll whisper incredibly naughty things in your ear— then I'll do them to you.

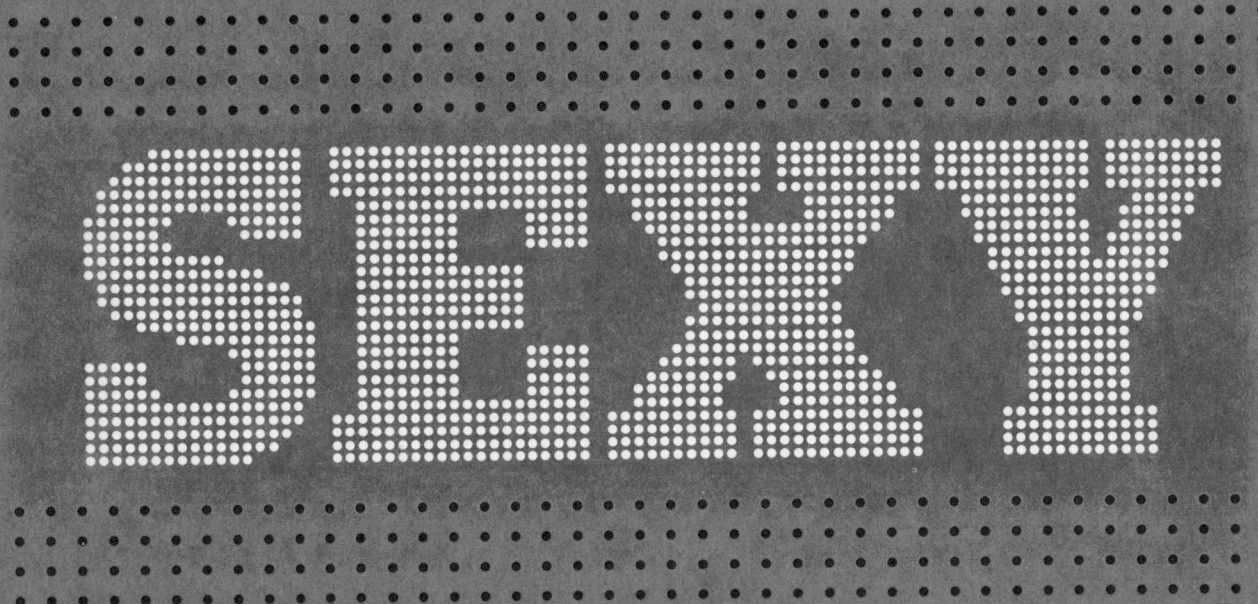

With this coupon, I'll tell you where to touch me and exactly how.

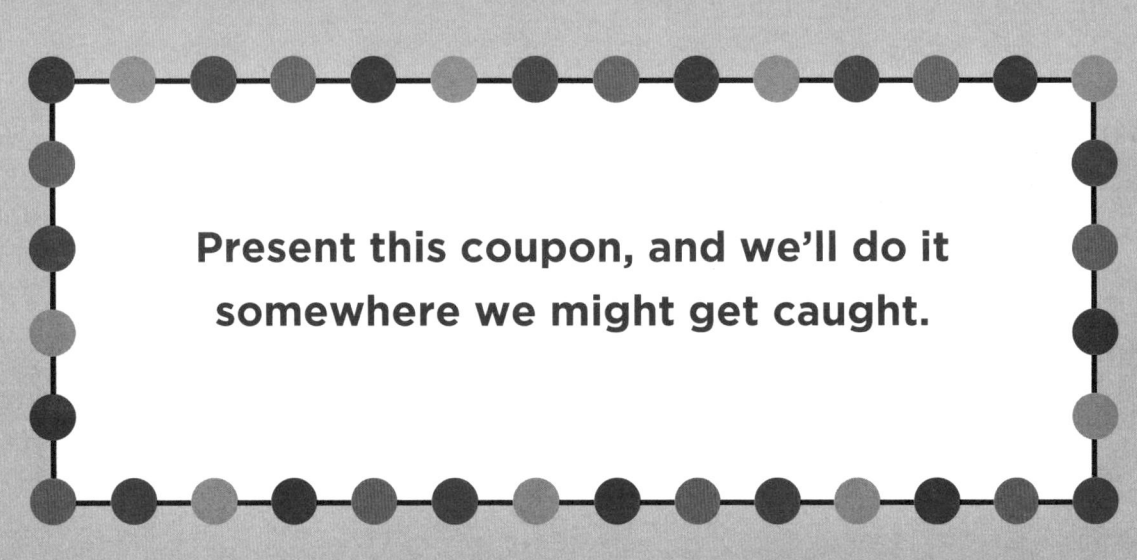

Present this coupon, and we'll do it somewhere we might get caught.

SEXY

This coupon is good for some naughty dessert. Watch as I lick whipped cream off of your most delicious areas.

Present this coupon, and we'll do a new position—one you've always wanted to do, but we've never tried.

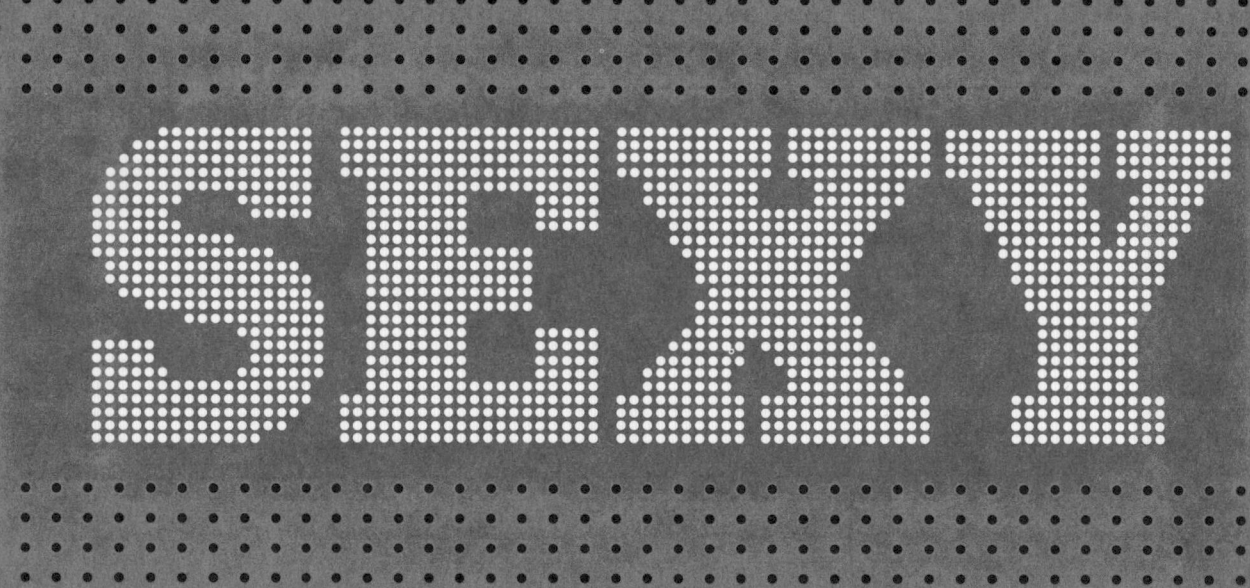

This coupon is redeemable for a romp in any room of your choice, with the lights on. I'll turn you on *and* light you up.

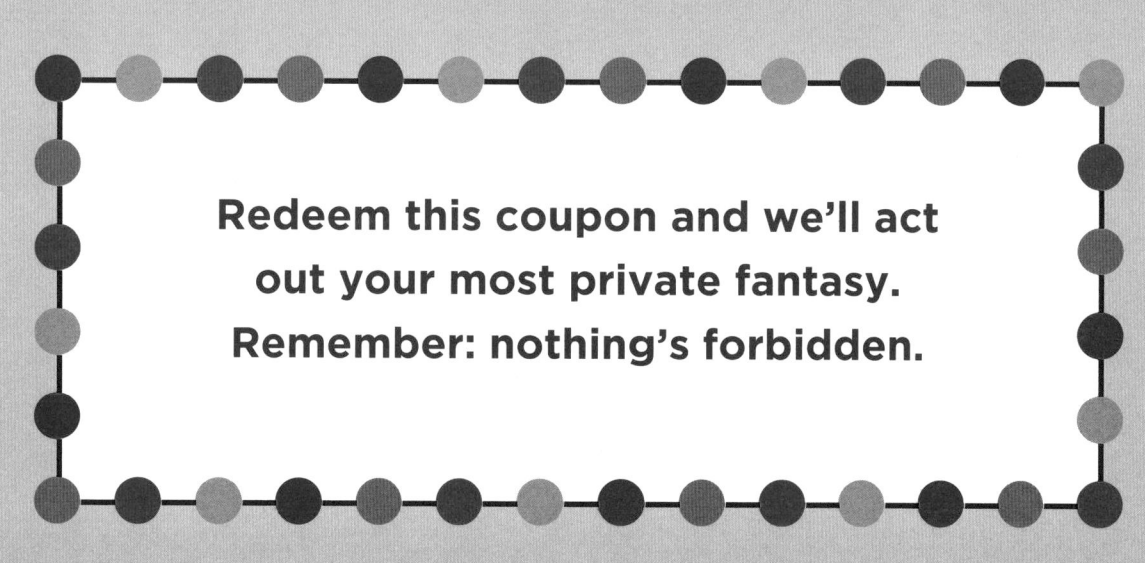

Redeem this coupon and we'll act
out your most private fantasy.
Remember: nothing's forbidden.

This coupon is good for a night of sexy views. Let's put up a mirror and watch ourselves in action.

Turn in this coupon and I'll take the lead. Just lie back and let me drive you wild.

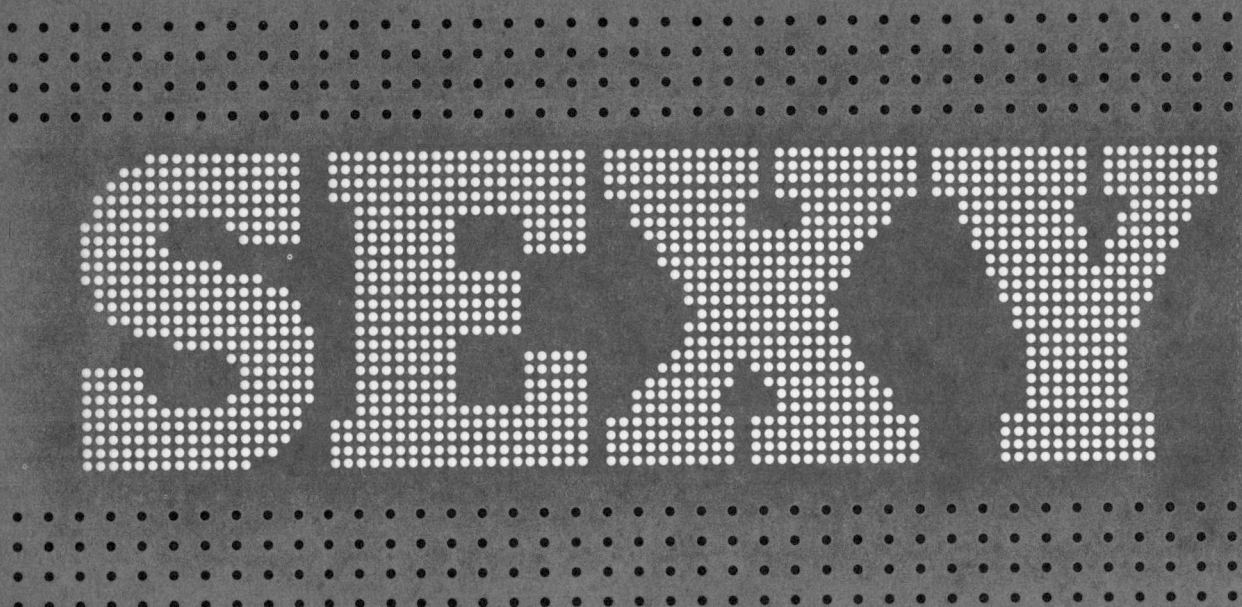

Redeem this coupon and we'll play good cop and naughty criminal—you bring the handcuffs.

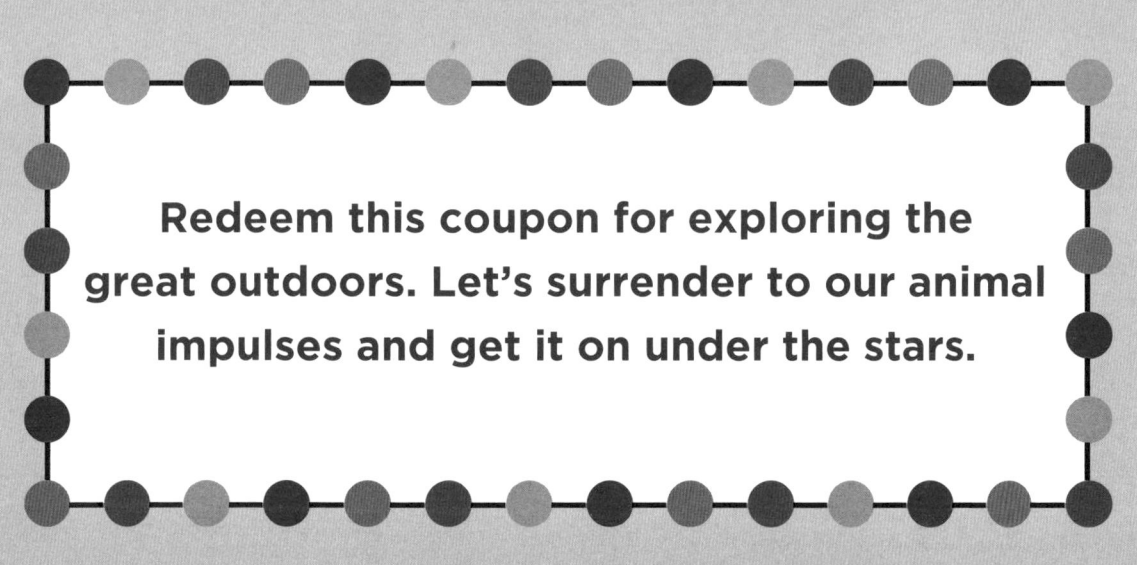

Redeem this coupon for exploring the great outdoors. Let's surrender to our animal impulses and get it on under the stars.

Turn in this coupon for a tantalizingly slow strip tease. You can look, but you'll have to wait until the grand finale to touch.

Redeem this coupon for some incredible oral action. I know exactly what to do to make you melt.

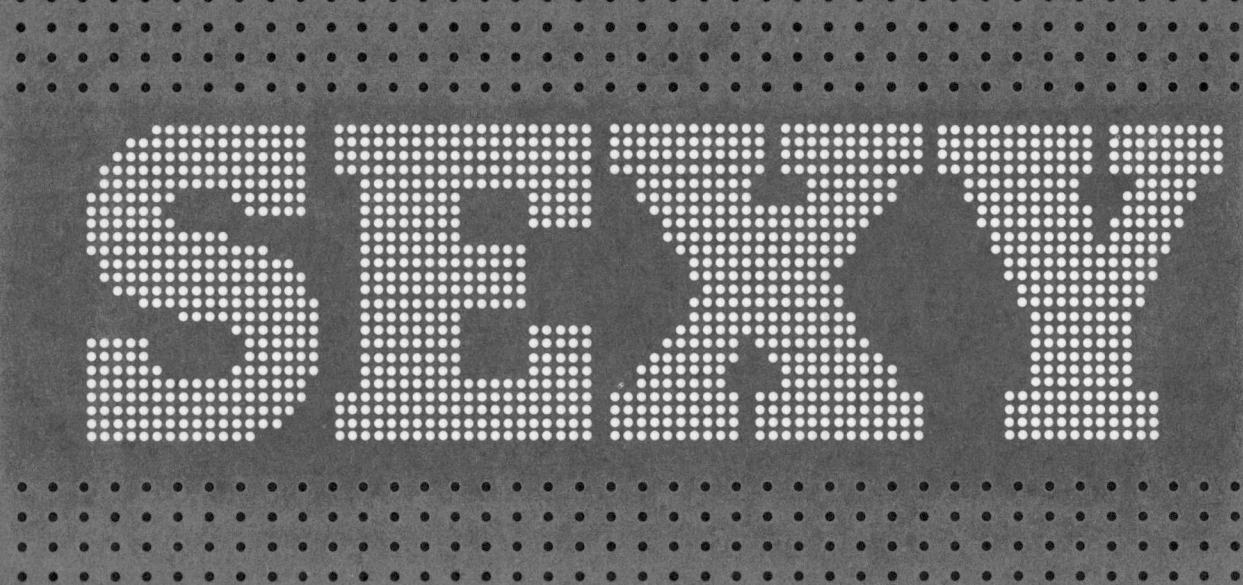

Turn in this coupon and I'll read you a naughty bedtime story. Then we'll reenact it.

Sext Me: This coupon is good for steamy text messages on a night when we're apart.

Present this coupon and we'll take a trip to the sex shop, where we can pick out some new sexy toys.

This coupon is good for one passionate, drop-everything quickie. Let's go!

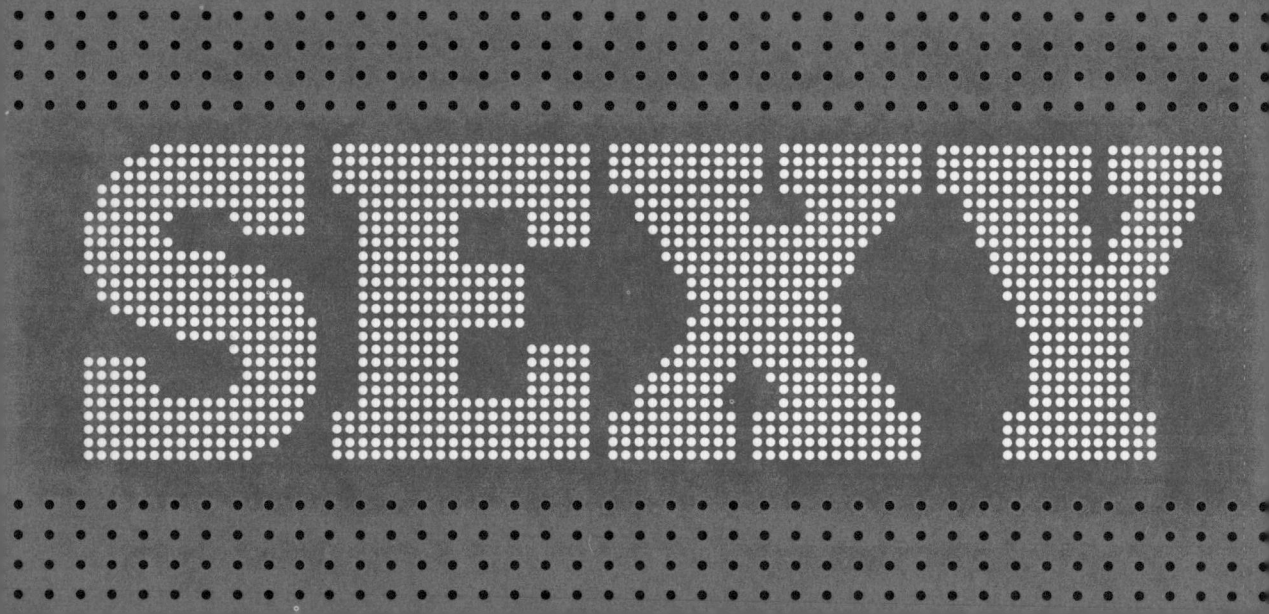

Present this coupon for a steamy shower scene. We'll give porn stars a run for their money with our moves!

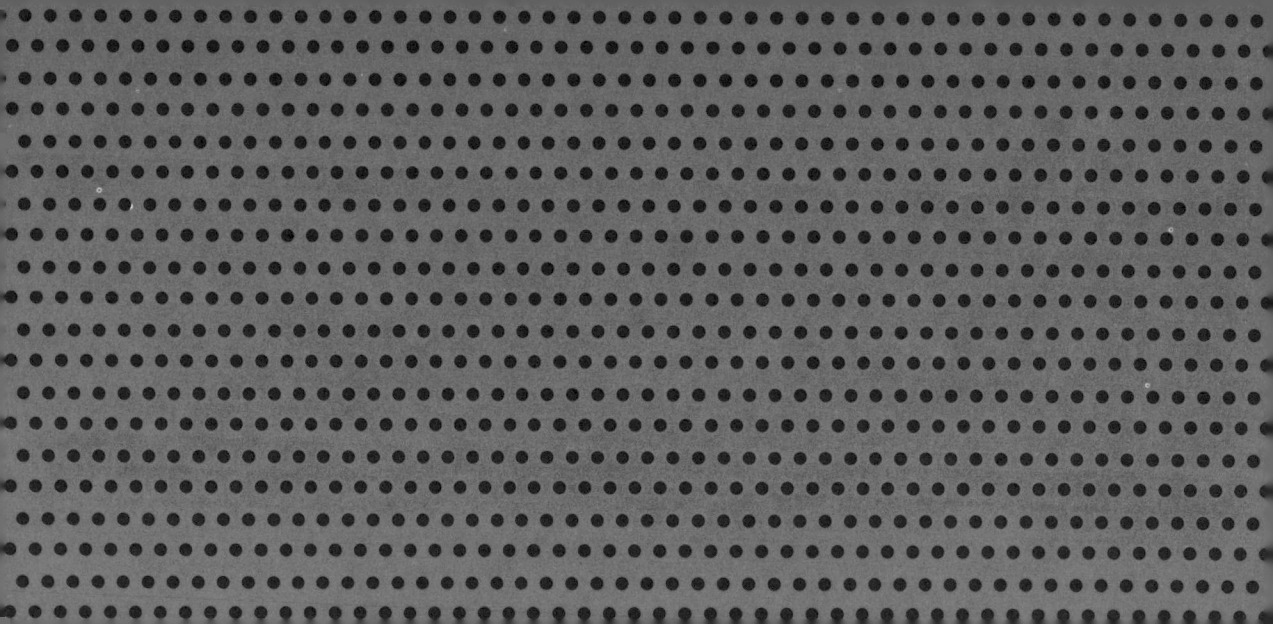

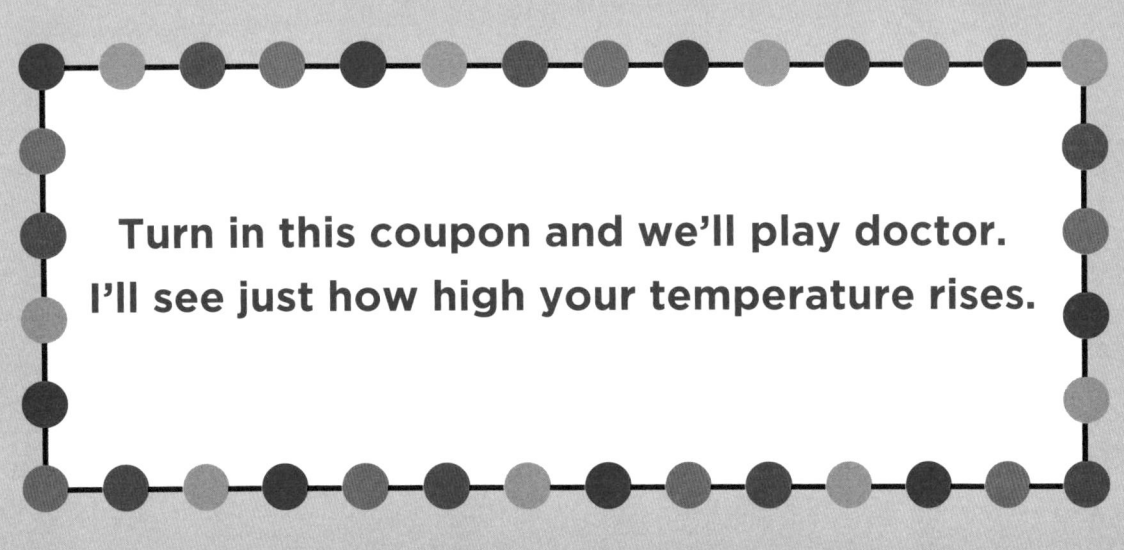

Turn in this coupon and we'll play doctor.
I'll see just how high your temperature rises.

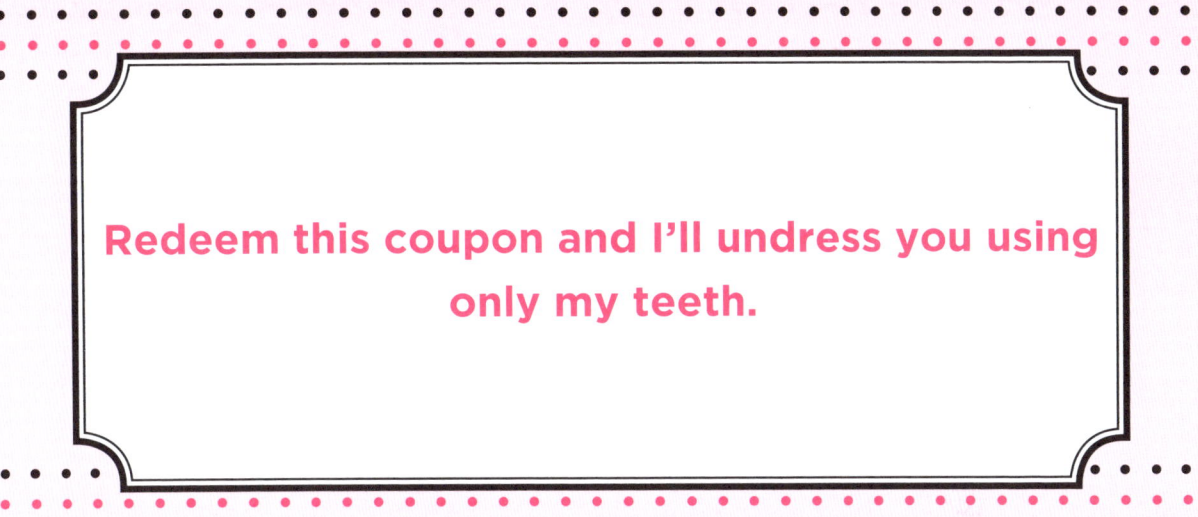

Redeem this coupon and I'll undress you using only my teeth.

Present this coupon when you want to be teased. Just watch me until you can't wait any longer.

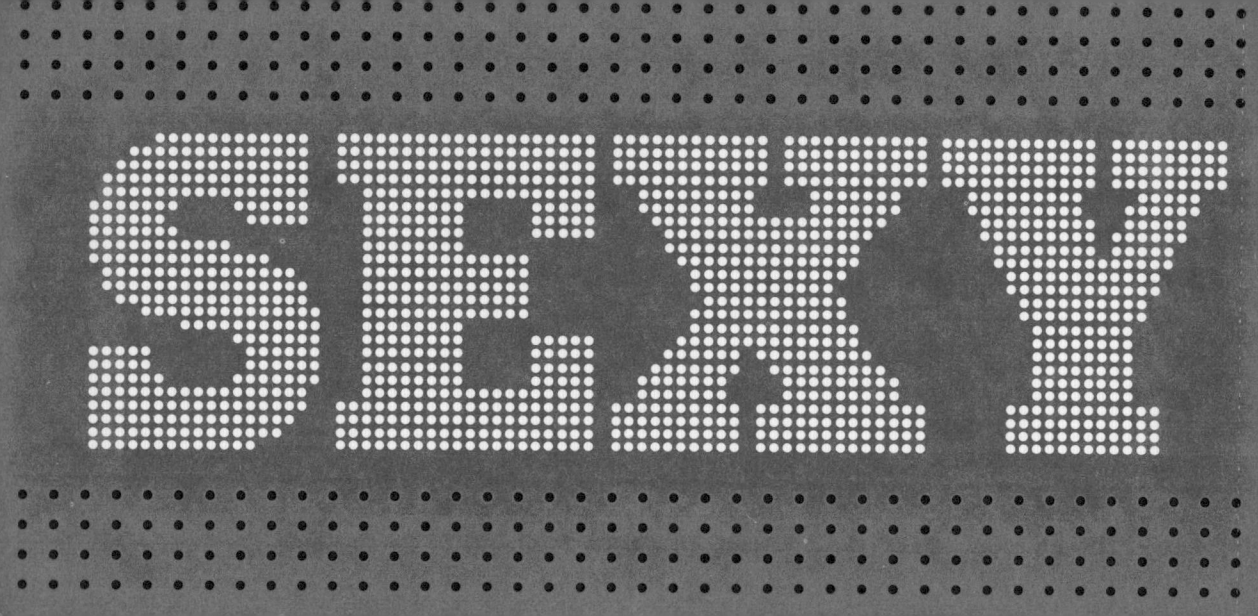